BASS-ICK THEORY

Volume 02: Conversations with Leroy
Detroit Edition

By Tony Muhammad

©Tony Muhammad 2021, San Diego, California

All rights reserved. No parts of this book may be used or reproduced in any manner without written permission from the author.

https://www.facebook.com/tony.muhammad.33

ISBN: 9781312019584

Table of Contents

Foreword 1
Preface 6
Introduction 8
Focus and Concentration 20
Music Listening Exercise 55
Quiet Time 68
Being successful as a musician 71
Conclusion 72
Afterword 74
Acknowledgments 80
Resources 81
Additional thanks to 81

Foreword

When Tony asked if I would write the Foreword for the second volume of Bass-ick Theory, I wondered what might best help his readers understand the author and the intent of the book. Daniel Brown does an excellent job describing Tony's music education and career in his Afterword. I know you will enjoy Daniel's insights, as I did, and you will learn many interesting things about Tony's experience. Eventually, I decided that sharing my experience of learning bass from him would offer a different perspective: Tony Muhammad the educator. I have considered myself extremely fortunate to be one of his students and secretly wished that everyone might have the opportunity that I have each week to learn from him.

Having played various instruments since age seven, when a friend asked me to join an impromptu musical ensemble for an upcoming event four years ago, it never occurred to me to say no. Creating music for people and being surrounded by the beauty of that music was something I loved. This group, however, had a guitarist and a drummer and was looking for a bassist. I had never touched a bass before, but our daughter had briefly taken lessons and we still had her bass. Her teacher seemed kind and patient, so I contacted him and asked if he would help me learn the three songs the group would play. Tony responded by saying, "Sure, easy stuff." I've since come to realize that he applies that description to most everything in life.

From the first moment I sat in the lesson room with Tony Muhammad, learning from him has been an extraordinary experience. You might not be surprised by this, as his personal philosophy is clearly described in his books. In our society, where people are guarded and too often cover their real selves with manufactured personae, it's unusual to find someone courageous and self-assured enough to be as authentic and vulnerable as he is in his writing. And in person, rarely does one encounter an instructor who pays such close attention, in order to see who you are, where you are, and what you need to move forward in your learning. Just as in his two books, Tony weaves personal stories into music theory and insights from a range of musicians to fill your being with a deep understanding of what being a musician, and more specifically, being a bassist, is all about. I was initially hooked when he said, "The bass is a spiritual instrument." Since then, he has given me innumerable reasons to love playing bass. Our lessons are an ongoing invitation to continually stretch myself by learning different music genres, technical aspects of playing, what the job of a bass player is, and how to use theory to intelligently and skillfully participate in creating music. And in some lessons, I barely touch my bass. Instead, we listen to specific recordings and he asks me to describe what I've heard. Slowly, my ear is improving and I'm able to pick up more nuances about the conversations the musicians are having with each other. Tony sees music as a conversation – this perspective magically transforms any performance into an intimate and meaningful interaction among musicians. The music theory Tony has shared with me has also deepened my love of music and my appreciation for how it's constructed. It is my hope that Tony's approach to music theory will also enhance your love of music and will help you enjoy the conversations inherent in the music you listen to, while deepening those you have with your fellow musicians.

I've also found that Tony never does things without an intention. As you read through the stories and exercises in this book, you can be assured that there is a reason why he has written them down for us. And not only is there serious thought preceding each of his decisions, I've never seen him make a decision that is self-serving. He holds a great love of humanity and frequently wears T-shirts that say things like, "Be a good human." As he describes in the book, Tony works diligently to be a better person each and every day. He also sees people clearly and accepts them for who they are. One frequent disagreement occurs when I argue that a person shouldn't be a certain way – and he steadfastly asserts that every person has a right to be who and what they want to be. This is not to say that he accepts the behavior of all people in his life. In fact, Tony has clear and consistent boundaries and only allows people with positive spirits to play a significant role in his life. When negativity or mean-spiritedness is offered in conversation, he simply informs the person that he has no interest in this. Amidst the increasing focus on mindfulness in our culture, Tony is the ultimate example of accepting the present moment while simultaneously taking full responsibility for the experience of his own life.

Because of his understated nature, it often surprises people when I tell them that Tony is one of the most generous people I know. He supports many people in his life, is a father figure to many younger men and women, and will always make time for people who are in need and are honestly trying to better themselves or their lives. He described the day he purchased groceries for a homeless man on the street as one of the best days of his life. This kindness and seriousness of purpose is balanced by a sense of humor that never quits. While our lessons are full of music and music theory, I have often left feeling that I've spent the entire time laughing.

Finally, I want to mention Tony's humility, as it permeates everything he does and how he does it. No matter what station in life a person holds, Tony treats everyone with respect and recognizes that he or she holds something for him to learn. His main goal as a musician was to be knowledgeable and skilled enough to be able to play with anyone – any group, any genre, any situation. While he has achieved that goal, he would never admit it. When offered a compliment, his usual response is, "I don't know anything about that." I've never heard him compare himself to others, criticize other musicians, or attempt to make himself look good in any situation. He simply shows up, does his job, and lets who he is speak for itself. You will see that philosophy reflected throughout the book; it is genuine, and something he lives every day of his life.

As someone who likes to learn but can be impatient with the process, I've occasionally wondered if another method might help me advance more quickly on my path to becoming a bassist. This has led me to purchase a variety of other music theory books for bassists. Each time one arrives, I enthusiastically pick it up, hoping it will fill the gaps in my understanding or teach me something I haven't learned yet. After a few hopeful days, I add it to the pile of other books that have not measured up. When I'm impatient with my progress, Tony reminds me that it's not the destination but the journey that is most important. Learning to play bass is comprised of so many exciting moments - understanding some piece of theory at a new or deeper level, feeling increasingly connected with my bass so it becomes an extension of the thoughts and music in my head, and using music as a form of authentic personal expression. He reminds me to enjoy each moment of this process, rather than wasting time being frustrated that I haven't reached a particular imagined destination. I appreciate that Tony's method, rich with the life experiences of so many musicians, textured by his orientation to music as a conversation, and sustained by his deep and strong foundation in music theory offers a continually interesting, multi-faceted approach to learning bass. May you find the books of this generous, knowledgeable, and thoughtful man to be as enriching for you as you continue along your own music journey.

-Helane Fronek, San Diego, California, July 2021

Helane Fronek, San Diego Bassist
Playing with Flex, May 29, 2021

Preface

"The two most powerful warriors are patience and time"
– Leo Tolstoy

I saw this quote as being most appropriate for this second edition of Bass-ick Theory. Yes, Tony has put together 20 new exercises to test the Bass player who is seeking the next level in his or her skill set. But what is so important here is the inward journey. Who better to help you with that than the infamous Leroy? Who has not had a Leroy in their lives? Either you grew up with him, went to school with him, worked with him, hired him, or he is one of your relatives. At some point you learned something from him in between laughing at him or being totally frustrated with him. Yet, if you are paying attention, he always has a deep message for you.

I see the message here as: grow personally from within, in order to open yourself to grow musically. Take note of all the great quotes from Tony's mentors, friends and fellow bass players who have attained these levels of skill. They got there by being *patient,* putting in the *time,* and paying attention and truly listening to Leroy.

I've got faith in all of you on your way to mastering those diminished or whole tone scales. Be at your best no matter what. Know it, study it, embrace it, FEEL IT!!!
Good Fortune, Peace and Blessings!

-Tony Thomas

Tony Thomas

Introduction

This book was written as a continuation of volume one. The response to the first volume helped me realize that there is a desire among bassists to improve their understanding of music theory and how to apply it, so they can create more pleasing bass lines and enjoy their instrument more. It is for this reason that I am offering Volume Two. There are twenty exercises in this edition that can contribute to overall better basic theory comprehension, which in turn could put a bassist/musician in a better situation to communicate and share the music that we all love. But becoming a musician is not all about music theory and practice. One road to discovering the pleasures of music and life that has worked for me has been to become a better human being overall. This is because, for me, life and music are one and the same. The positive energies that can be experienced while playing or creating music can also be experienced during our daily lives. Once I was able to realize this, I created a personal contract to hold myself accountable every day. Not only did I sign the contract, but I placed it in a plastic sleeve and taped it to a mirror that I see every day. I share this contract with you below and believe that, if you decide to design one for yourself, you will immediately see the benefits. Some of my friends just copied my contract and plugged in their name, which is fine by me.

*Today is a great day.
You are alive and healthy.
You have a wonderful smile, please share it with everyone you meet today.
Please remind yourself that you are blessed.
Take care of yourself and all others you encounter. If you have the opportunity to help someone today, do it without hesitation.
Be mindful of what you eat, what you think, what you do, and what you say.*

This volume is also different in a couple of ways. One way that comes to mind is the character Leroy. Once again, I should mention that, even though Leroy is a fictitious character, we all know him as a real life person somewhere in our circle of friends, co-workers, family, etc. Most of the theoretical responses in this book will come by way of conversations with Leroy. And, as we know, sometimes Leroy will give an answer right on the money. Sometimes he will give an answer that you will have to think about a bit and maybe do some work to actually understand what he was saying. And sometimes the answer he will give will make you wish that you never asked him a question at all. If that happens, I will jump in and attempt to clarify or patch up whatever mess Leroy created. Another thing you will notice is in the dedication. This book is dedicated to Reginald Canty and the Detroit Bass Players. I came across Reginald on social media, Facebook to be exact. From time to time, he would post extremely nice bass solos. On one particular occasion when I noticed that Reginald had posted a solo, I didn't have my Bluetooth speaker and got distracted, and I said to myself, "I already know it's a great solo, so I'll listen to it a little bit later." When I finally got the Bluetooth speaker and listened to the solo, I knew I needed to reach out to this brother for REELZ. This solo stood out even more than the other great solos of his I had listened to.

The Detroit Bass player group is very large, and I've enjoyed getting to know many bassists who are part of it. However, there are a few members that I would like to give a special shout out to as a result of recent telephone conversations. After speaking with these people, I found myself bumping into walls due to the positive energy that came from these conversations. I was amazed at the energy they had and how they said my book made them feel. Some of these people include Reginald Canty, Michael Rais, Alfred Shorter, Mary J. Morgan, Kevin Nowak, Marilee Benore, Jeff Dalton, Gordon Pfeiffer, Gwenyth Hayes and Ralph Armstrong - the list goes on and on.

"Greetings Bass Family! I'd like to point out that music is also a language, and the bass is the foundation in most music of the western culture. It would be difficult to find any music in western or pop culture that didn't have a bass, or an instrument serving that function. My search goes all the way back to Domenico Dragonetti, a three string Double bassist who created bass prominence in music. Playing Double Bass in the Gregorian chants sung in church, he was the principal musician in the early Catholic Church - not the organ or the choir. Previous to that, the Bassist just copied the cello line. I credit him for the prominence bass holds in modern music today. From this observation and many others, I've learned that the role of a bassist (IMHO) is to help give any piece of music the propulsion it needs to convey the needed message! It is important to observe what the lead instrument is doing, be it voice or instrument, and to decipher whether that instrument is creating or releasing tension, at which point the bassist should react accordingly. It is the job of the bassist to accurately display the dynamics of any piece of music, moment by moment, which in turn would make the music appear seamless!!!

My friends, we are global ambassadors of good will whose only purpose is to bring pleasure to those who listen. Understood by all, regardless of any language barrier, it's our job to make that music sound and feel good! THAT is your badge and your crown. I wear mine proudly!!

"Talkin bout dat Bass !!!!!"

—Reginald Canty

Reginald Canty, Detroit Bassist

"This is dedicated to all musicians.

As a music educator, I teach middle school in Metro Detroit. One of the most important topics that I feel students need to learn is to improvise. When I teach my students about improvisation, I get students that become really worried because they don't know what to do. They are not sure what to play and feel like they will make mistakes. The thing is, they actually do know how to improvise. It is important for all musicians to listen and play what feels right to them. I give them ideas to use, such as grooves, a list of notes from scales and then give them time to jam along with recorded tracks. At first, they are playing around with ideas. The next step is for all of them to try their ideas with the track. Now I can see that things are starting to click with them. Their eyes light up, they start to play more and really start to speak. They are starting to feel the groove and music! This goes on for most of the class period. As they become more comfortable with improvisation, they want to keep going and talk with each other through their instrument. We must do this with our instruments as much as we work on technique, scales and rhythms. This allows us to really get to be more fluent on our instrument and help learn the language of music."

-Michael Rais

Michael Rais, Detroit Bassist and Music Educator

"The Bass is an instrument that has a fascinating history. A lot of people who play it do not know that the bass is a religious instrument. It is the original religious instrument of the Catholic church. Most Gregorian chants were written for the bass. It was the instrument that was used by the monks in the monasteries. Some had 3 strings, while others had 7 or 8 strings. One thing I learned from over 50 years of playing is that bass players put too much emphasis on equipment! The sound comes from your fingers and the left hand technique. The very first person to explain the science of the left hand technique to me was James Jamerson. He showed me that the thumb and the second finger should be in line when you move the hand all over the finger board, like a vice.

This technique was invented in 1870 by Josef Harbes. He invented the 12 positions that we use today. This is the way James Jamerson played his bass. Myself, Ron Carter, Chuck Rainey, Stanley Clarke and many master bass players play this way, too. Case in point!! I saw James Jamerson play a Hofner Beetle bass!!! He sounded like James Jamerson. When he finished playing, he looked at me and said in his deep voice, 'I play the notes - no funny sounds, because I know the Technique.'"

-Ralph Armstrong

Ralph Armstrong, Detroit Bassist

Have you ever checked out a bass player that is really grooving and you notice that he might be wearing a really cool hat? My closest compadres and I have a long running joke about hats. Sometimes I wear different hats just to walk around the house, not even going outside. I'm not really sure what that is all about, but it happens. Here's a list of some of the hats I have worn at one time or another. Some of them I try not to wear any longer, but I will admit that they have been worn at one time or another. I will use acronyms to give specific details about the hats.

FBP - Frustrated Bass Player
IBP - Impatient Bass Player
ABP - Angry Bass Player
IBP - Intimidated Bass Player
SBP - Selfish Bass Player

These are the ones I prefer to wear these days
DBP - Dedicated Bass Player {Detroit Bass Player}
KBP - Kind Bass Player
CBP - Compassionate Bass Player
CBP - Confident Bass Player

In 2009, I was kind of watching a movie entitled Handsome Harry, although I was not really into it. A scene came on where a band was playing at a party. Once I heard the tone of the bass player, I realized that the tone was very familiar. At that point, I began to pay more attention to the movie. When they showed a close up of the band, I noticed the red hat that the bassist was wearing. A closer look showed me that it was Bill Dotts, out of Harlem in New York, my good friend of more than 35 years. He was wearing the red hat that he had picked out on his visit here to San Diego. Bill is a serious Bass player hat aficionado. He's even been known to wear a construction hat, and he does not work construction. All of this is to say, "Be aware of the hat you wear, because there are those of us that can see you."

Bill Dotts, NYC Bassist

Focus and Concentration

Focus and concentration are both very important parts of becoming a solid, well-rounded bassist. Your concentration can be improved in several ways. One way that I use on a regular basis is to commit myself to the present moment. When I find myself thinking about anything besides what I'm practicing or playing, I try to let those thoughts go and return to what I'm actually doing. Then, once you feel solid and grounded and if you are practicing alone, listen to yourself. Listen to your tone and listen to your attack on the notes you choose to play. When you play a note that you didn't intend to play, is it a bad note? Is it a note that you just happened to stumble on? What is the note? How does it relate to the chord? I know many bass players who, once they hit a note that they did not intend to play, stop playing and go into self-correction mode in order to stay in total control. Trying to remain in total control is an impediment to really playing bass. I have learned that once you relax and allow the music to flow through you as if you are a conduit, you will be able to enjoy the experience and the music you're creating just as much as the listeners do. Your musical awareness will increase, and you will be able to handle just about anything that comes your way. In that case you might find that the note you used to stumble on is actually a flat 9 or sharp 9 or sharp 11 - just an altered note that adds some tension. One reason you might have stumbled upon these notes is that you've heard them in the music of people like Charlie Parker, Dizzy Gillespie, and definitely Jaco. This provides a model in your head, and you naturally play those notes even when you didn't intend to. By paying attention to what the note was and how it relates to what you're playing, you'll gain greater understanding and be able to relax more into what comes out of you when you play.

"Do your homework and be prepared."

Christopher Barrick, Professor of Music
Detroit Saxophonist and Bassist

Now that we've gotten the more difficult part out of the way, let's get to the fun part: having fun, and especially having fun on your gig. Remember that this is what we all love to do, play bass, right? There are certain musicians that I really enjoy playing with because we provide the music required for the occasion, but higher on our list is having a good time. We all have our strengths and weaknesses, and one of my weaknesses is laughter. Once I start laughing, that's all she wrote. That's it. A very good friend and master pianist, Kevin Flournoy, can make anyone on the planet laugh. It could be with just eye contact, or the way he unnecessarily positions his arm to play one note. Kevin is the person who INTRODUCED me to Leroy. Being on stage with Kevin and Leroy is way too much trouble. The thing I should mention is that both Kevin and Leroy are master musicians, but Kevin is also a master of the straight face. Kevin and Leroy have gotten me into trouble where all the attention ends up on me, because Kevin can change immediately to a serious straight face, and Leroy will just continue to look like Leroy. Then, guess what we have at that point? Tony is the only one laughing and it looks like I'm the only culprit. At certain points during the gig, I look straight ahead and refuse to look in either of their directions, because they continue to cut up. Over the last few years both Kevin and Leroy have gotten me into lots of trouble on gigs. Kevin's also been known to get me into trouble even when Leroy's not on the gig by switching to a guitar patch on his keyboard, playing a guitar lick, and then telling me that was Leroy on the gig and that I need to pay him. Or he would come up with excuses for Leroy missing the gig and mention that Leroy still expects to be paid. Ok, the point I'm getting at here is to relax and have fun.

I should mention that Kevin and Leroy are very good friends. Leroy often travels on tour with Kevin. Most of the time pictures can tell at least 1,000 words. The next picture proves that point.

Kevin Flournoy (AKA K-Flow),
West Coast Pianist/Producer

Exercise # 1 Melodic minor scale harmony

The melodic minor scale is a fun scale to play, and it will also introduce you to several new chords to add to your list of chords you can use. Please learn this scale and all of the modes and chords that can be built from the modes. It would be easy to memorize the melodic minor scale by thinking of a major scale with a lowered 3rd. Let's stick with A as our starting note, because this will help you learn the theory better. While starting with C makes it easier for you to immediately pick up the scale because of the natural half steps, playing the A scale will help you really understand how the scale is constructed.

A melodic minor scale: A B C D E F# G# A

A *minor/Major chord* can be constructed by using the root, 3rd, 5th and 7th.

Root → minor 3rd → Major 3rd → Major 3rd

In the A melodic minor scale, this chord will be A C E G#. This will be an unusual sound to your ears at first, but as you continue to play the scale and chord, your ears will adjust. This chord gets its name from the fact that the interval from the root to the 3 is a minor 3rd, and from the root to the 7 is a Major 7th.

The 2nd mode of this scale starts on B: B C D E F# G# A B
Using the Root, b2nd/b9th, 4th and 5th you can create a *Suspended (sus) b9 chord:* B, E, F# C
The sus chord has a 4 instead of a 3, so it's 1 – 4 – 5 and you add the b9 at the top. You can also add the 7 so the chord is made up of: 1 4 5 7 b9.

The 3rd mode starts on C: C D E F# G# A B C
This scale is sometimes called a *Lydian augmented scale* because it has a #4 and a #5.

The 4th mode starts on D: D E F# G# A B C D
This scale is sometimes called a *Lydian dominant scale* because you can build a dominant chord and also utilize the #4.

The 5th mode starts on E: E F# G# A B C D E
This scale can be used to create a minor/Major chord and *slash chords*. You will see many slash chords where the pianist is playing a triad and prefers the bass to play a different note against the chord. If there is not a bassist, the pianist may play that note with the left hand to get the same effect.

The 6th mode starts on F#: F# G# A B C D E F#
This scale is sometimes called a *half diminished scale* or *Locrian # 2*. You can use it in just about the same ways as the Locrian scale from the Major scale harmony.

The 7th mode starts on G#: G# A B C D E F# G#
This is sometimes called a *diminished/whole tone scale* because the 1st half is diminished, and the 2nd half is whole tone. This scale is also used to create altered dominant 7th chords, because every possible alteration that you might use is already in this scale. By looking at the scale above, you can see that it has a b9, #9, b5, #5, #11, and b13.

Exercise # 2   Contrasting minor 7th and minor/Major chords

This exercise would be to switch back and forth between a minor 7th chord and a minor/Major chord. Nate Brown or Michael Rais will give you an idea of what this should sound like via YouTube or via their personal website. (Please see the Resources Page at the back of this book.) Nate also has a very nice original tune of his that has a section where the tune switches from minor to minor/Major.

Exercise # 3   Chords and possible extensions

Use your metronome or drum machine with a nice swinging beat and arpeggiate the chords below, along with each extension listed in parentheses. Be sure to play each arpeggio ascending and descending. Play very slowly and then gradually increase the speed. The name of the chord tells you what notes the chord is built from.

A Maj 7 [9, #11, #13] – the 9 is the octave of the 2. #11 is the octave of #4, and #13 is the octave of #6.
First, play the A Maj 7 chord ascending and descending. Then do the same for AMaj 9, AMaj 7 #11, and AMaj 7 #13. With each extension, you only add that extra note at the top, so the AMaj 7 #13 does not include the 9 or #11.

AMaj6 [9, #11] – this chord is composed of R–3–5–6 only. After you have played this ascending and descending, add each of the extensions.

A minor/Major [9, 11, 13] - this is the same chord as in Exercise #1, with the extensions added.

Exercise # 4   More chords to add to your repertoire

Again, set your metronome or drum machine to a nice swinging beat and arpeggiate the chords below, along with each extension listed in parentheses. Play each arpeggio ascending and descending. Start slowly and gradually increase the speed.

A minor 6 [9, 11]

A minor 7 [9, 11, 13]

A minor 7 b5 [9, 11, 13]

"People don't realize the importance of a good solid bass player. A good bassist is someone that can lead or follow, whatever the musical situation calls for. Like the human body, you need a strong backbone - that's what makes bass so important in a setting. Bass players are like eyebrows - you don't notice them until they are gone."

Gordon Pfeiffer, Detroit Bassist

Very early in my bass endeavors I had the chance to ask Leroy what I should practice in order to become a better bassist. I can remember it as if it were yesterday. "Hey Leroy, can I ask you a serious question?" He did not answer right away, so I waited a few seconds and asked again. This time, he looked at me and said, "What?" So, I asked again, "What should I work on to get better?" Then, he looked at me and asked, "Why?" I was starting to get frustrated, so for the second time, I said, "Because I want to be a better bass player." Then I said, "Never mind, man, you know what????" Leroy then said, "Hey young blood, you better watch your tone." At that point I got nervous because usually, when someone tells you to watch your tone, a fight might be coming your way. Leroy has been known to have been in quite a few fist fights, so I just took a step back. Then he said, "Hey Lil' hommie, did you hear me?" It was only then that I got the message he was conveying. He was referring to my bass tone.

"When we are open to learning or attaining wisdom, our practice does not end, it continues to deepen."

Leroy
Bassist, unknown location

Exercise # 5   More chords

Play these two chords and the extensions below. Listen to what each chord and the altered notes in the extensions sound like.

A diminished 7

A Dominant 7 [b9, 9, #11, b13, 13]

Exercise # 6   Focusing on the rhythms

Take a piece of sheet music that you are totally unfamiliar with and thoroughly study the rhythms. After internalizing the rhythms, clap them in time. Take notice of the time signature and find a random tune with the same time signature. Now, play this tune and clap the rhythms from the original tune against this new tune. Change tempo by picking a faster or slower tune, or change the genre of the music, but stay committed to the rhythms on the chart.

Exercise # 7   Observing intervals.

Again, select a piece of music that you are unfamiliar with. Now, this time select two, three or four measures of this material. Sing the intervals that you see in the measures. After singing what you imagine the melody should sound like, take a listen to the music and check to see how close you came to the actual melody. This will give you a huge advantage when looking at music that you have not heard prior to attempting to play it.

"The bass is the foundation of all music. Locking in a solid groove entices people to feel free to move in the way they feel most natural and comfortable."

Hugh Bray, Detroit Bassist

What I have grown to notice is that every person you meet will either treat you according to the energy you present or bring with you, or they will treat you with the energy that they have accumulated, or a combination of both of these options. If you are blessed with the gift of being a musician or artist, let the energy from your person and instrument introduce you.

"With some people, it's very easy to see what values they bring to the world."

AntMo, San Diego Bassist

Leroy has been frequently labeled as a walking contradiction. Known at times to exercise patience, compassion, humanity, and wisdom, he is a person who sees and understands what other people don't understand. I was able to get this picture of him at the airport. I'm sure you can see the compassion and other traits of his personality in the photo on the next page, but what the picture does not tell you is that he has already missed his flight. It left 40 minutes earlier.

Everything has its own natural rhythm. When you are the bass player in your group or combo, listening to rhythms is extremely important and can provide the fuel you use for survival. Once you provide the bottom support, open your ears. I've heard this called having "big ears." Take time to listen to each instrument individually, seeing how they intertwine with each other. (See Bass-ick Theory volume one, Exercise #14 and the section on Feel pp.45-47 for more explanation and ways to practice this.) Sometimes it's what you don't hear that's most important. If you hear an interesting rhythm, listen to see if it is repeated. If you find it unique, maybe you can play something similar, then create eye contact with the musician who played it as an acknowledgement that you heard it or liked it. That might inspire him or her to play it again - or maybe you play it together. A lot of times these kinds of gestures help to unite the band. Take a minute to listen to some of the outro's that some groups play. Paying attention to the rhythms can also help you keep your place.

"I believe in leaving space to let the music breathe. Sometimes what you don't play is just as important as what you do."

Gwenyth Hayes, Detroit Bassist

"Music is organized sound and silence"

William Hayes, Detroit Bassist

I remember being in a recording session with Greg Grainger, and when we got to the bridge of the tune, I was playing ahead of the beat. Greg, being the excellent timekeeper that he is, just made eye contact with me, then he looked at his cymbal and looked back at me. This caused me to look at the cymbal. I saw the time he was keeping on the cymbal and pulled myself right back in time. Greg has continued to be a huge positive force in my life. We have taken many road trips where we would be listening to music for hours and he'd suddenly ask me, "Hey Antmo, where's the one? What's the time signature?" Sometimes I'd try to change the subject, but it never worked. He would answer the question I'd asked and get right back to his question.

Greg Grainger, Drummer

"A cup a day helps keep mistakes away."

Mary J Morgan, NYC Bassist

One evening I decided to stop by The Jazz Joint to listen to my good friend and fellow bass player, Alfred Shorter. When I got there, the first set was about mid-way finished. As usual, Al was chopping off heads with his funky grooves. We laugh and joke a lot and I've told Al that I truly believe something is seriously wrong with him, because it's not normal for a person to continue to create grooves that funky.

Leroy was on the gig with Al. Leroy took a serious solo on the last tune of the set. At the end of the set, I went up to Al and told him that I really enjoyed his playing, as usual. We began the normal, "How you been?" And "Wazzzz up!" Then Leroy joined us. I was not personally in the mood to deal with Leroy, because I just wasn't feeling that right now, so I said a few words to him and then continued to chat with Al. Al mentioned to Leroy that he really dug the solo he took. Al subsequently asked Leroy what he was thinking about when he took the solo, and I thought to myself, "Here we go." When Al asked Leroy, Leroy didn't answer right away. After a long pause, Leroy told Al that during that solo he was thinking about the gravitational pull of the earth and several seagulls. Al had a look on his face that you could write a book about. It started to feel very awkward as Al continued to look at Leroy with this indescribable expression on his face. After what seemed like a very long time, Al said to Leroy while nodding his head, "Leroy, I appreciate you trying to help me." After Leroy left, Al and I continued to talk and then I mentioned to Al that, from what I heard, Leroy was playing a series of triads from a diminished scale over a dominant chord.

"Music is a journey. All you have to do is be willing to take the twists and the curves along with the ups and downs."

Alfred Shorter, Detroit Bassist

Exercise # 8   The Leroy diminished thing

Let's start out with the A dominant 7th chord that Leroy was soloing over: *A C# E G*

Next, let's write out the A half-step/whole step diminished scale that Leroy was using. There are two types of diminished scales: a half step/whole step scale (which alternates half and whole steps beginning with a half step) and a whole step/half step scale (which alternates half and whole steps beginning with a whole step).

The half step/whole step scale is: A *Bb C Db Eb E F# G A*
When you look at this scale there's a series of Major and minor triads that are naturally in this scale. The series of triads are based off of successive minor thirds.

A C# E (Major triad) and *A C E (minor triad) are* the first set. Then if you go up a minor 3rd you will see *C E G* (Major triad) and *C Eb G (minor triad)*. Continue up another minor third and you will see *Eb G Bb* (Major triad) and *Eb Gb Bb (minor triad)*.

The final set of triads you will see is *F# A# C# (Major triad)* and *F# A C# (minor triad)*. All of these Major and minor triads can be found naturally in this diminished scale. What Leroy was doing was toggling back and forth between these triads. This was one of the masterful things that Jazz Great John Coltrane was known for. After explaining this to my good friend Al, I saw a genuine smile as tons of ideas went off in his head. Al gave me a fist bump, then we continued with the multitude of jokes and funny stuff that we always stumble on every time we hang out.

These exercises can actually end up being excellent choices to add to your musical arsenal, and you can make them fun to play. The more you practice, the more fun you will have and the things you practice will begin to come out naturally in your playing.

"A beginner wonders how loud he/she has to play so everyone else can hear them. A pro wonders how quiet he/she has to play so he can hear everyone else."

Randy Streicher, Detroit Bassist
"Practice, listen and play what the music requires."

Thomas Shell, Detroit Bassist

There's a Jazz festival in Denver that we play each year. One year in particular stands out more than others. I received the email with the travel itinerary as usual, and when I looked at the group email, I noticed that Leroy's name was included. That was interesting because I knew that Leroy did not have a valid email address anywhere to be found. I took it upon myself to take a drive over to his auntie's house where he was last residing to give him the info. I kind of anticipated a problem because the flight was scheduled to leave BWI at 0645 hours. I could not see Leroy making that flight, especially since TSA was enforcing a two hour pre-flight check-in. Once I arrived at Leroy's, it wasn't a big shock to find that he was not at home. I spoke to his auntie and gave her the flight information. She could tell from the look on my face that I really didn't think Leroy could make the flight that early. She tried to reassure me by saying, "Tone, don't worry. I'll have him sitting on the front porch with his guitar and his baggage waiting for you." I really wanted to believe her, so I simply said, "Ok thanks," but I really didn't believe that Leroy would be ready. I drove home and went to bed extra early because, with travel time and the two hour early check-in, I needed to be up around 3am. Early next morning as I approached the 700 block of Roundview Rd, the street was dark and only a few porches had lights on. As I got closer to his place, I could see the silhouette of what appeared to be a male. I saw a guitar case and a very small suitcase. Then I could see Leroy. As I got closer, I could smell the bacon from his favorite bacon and egg sandwich that he was eating. I said, "Good morning," but he did not answer. I mentioned that I spoke with his auntie and gave her the flight info. He still didn't say anything. As I was explaining to him about the early bird check-in, he completely ignored me. When he did say something, he only said, "Do what you must," which was completely unrelated to the topic we were discussing. Other than that, he didn't say anything during the entire ride to the airport. Once we checked in and got our seats on the plane, he ordered a cocktail. While sipping the cocktail, he pulled out a chart for a tune entitled "Watch What Happens" by Michel Legrand. He continued to just stare at the chart, so I stared at it too. I wasn't really getting too much out of it, so eventually I asked him why he was continuing to stare at the chart. He said, "Look at the first four measures. What do you see?" I replied, "I see EbMaj7 for two bars and F9 for two bars." Then, Leroy asked me how those chords were related, and I said, "They are a whole step away from each other is all I know." With frustration he said, "That's what's wrong with you new cats. You don't know anything about anything. All y'all do is follow the chords." Then he asked me what the notes were in each chord, and I replied that they were Eb G Bb D and F A C Eb G. He then told me to look at the common notes and look for notes that are a half step apart. As I saw two common notes and notes a half step apart, the light bulbs started to go off in my head. Then he asked me about the next four measures. I described the sequence of F9 / F-9 / Bb7 / EbMaj / EMaj7 / FMaj7 / EMaj7 and then the repeat. He explained that whenever you see a Dominant chord and it is followed by a weaker chord with the same root, that's a signal that a key change is coming. So F9 followed by F-9 and then Bb7 is a signal that you are heading to the key of EbMaj. Then he asked me about the 2nd ending, which was

EbMaj7 / EMaj7 / FMaj7 / F#Maj7 leading up to GMaj7.

This time I could see the chromatic walk up. The GMaj7 was followed by G-7 and C7, so this time I knew that we were going to the key of FMaj. After this, my head was spinning, and I continued to look at the rest of the tune. I wanted to ask questions about the melody, but he stopped talking to me completely, ordered another cocktail, and then went to sleep. When we eventually landed in Denver, I was still studying chord progressions, and Leroy was seriously snoring.

"What Key ????"

Daniel Speights, Detroit Bassist

Exercise # 9   Augmented chords

Take time to practice augmented chords, which are constructed as follows:

Root → Major 3rd → Major 3rd

They have a distinct sound being there's a raised 5th.
The A augmented chord consists of *A C# E#*
Practice them around the circle of 4ths or moving in thirds. Once your ears have adjusted to the sound of the raised 5th, you will be able to decide what you should play when you see this chord in the music.

I know a few bassists that try to arpeggiate every single chord they see on the chart. This not only does not add to the music, but it can become a nuisance to the other musicians. It might be a good idea to just listen. Maybe the vocalist is singing that altered note of the chord in the melody. Maybe the saxophone player is playing that note. Always try to be mindful when involved in a musical situation: listen, listen again, and then when you finish, listen some more. I remember a situation where we had a guitarist and a pianist who were not able to play together because they didn't listen to each other. When the music called for a specific chord, they both automatically just played the entire chord, so they created a duplicate of every chord. Finally, I suggested that maybe one of them could just play melodic shapes instead of playing the chord. This suggestion worked for all of one gig, and after that, the one with the biggest ego decided to leave the band. That's when Leroy was invited to join the band. There is a spiritual poet back east who goes by the name of the "the last Don." He claims that Leroy is a musical disciple who writes scriptures of music. I don't know about all that. As a matter of fact, I don't know about **any** of that!!!!!!

The Last Don, East Coast Poet

"You are never too old to learn to play bass"

Marilee Benore, Detroit Bassist

Sometimes I have difficulty admitting this, but when I think of guitar, I think of Leroy. Even with all the other stuff that comes with Leroy, he always delivers. This is a direct example of something my friend Milt shared with me a long time ago. I can still clearly remember him mentioning to me that people don't choose the instrument to play, the instrument chooses the person. He went on to say that he only had two jobs in his lifetime. The first was delivering newspapers. But Milt was fortunate to discover who he was very early in his life, and once he realized he was a musician – a bassist – he never held another job. He said he had a very early interest in music and his mother bought him a violin and got him violin lessons. Shortly after learning to play the violin, he said the bass chose him, so he decided to ask his mother for a bass. What I'm about to share with you is something that I've noticed many, many times over. The instrument that a person chooses is often times a reflection of their personality. Sometimes it's a good fit, and sometimes maybe not. What I quickly observe is the awareness of individuals. At times I notice that some musicians are not aware that they are not aware. This is not a judgment. This is not a good thing, nor a bad thing, it's just a thing that is. I am about to give you two perfect examples of what I am trying to say here.

The first one is in reference to a bassist here on the west coast, right here in San Diego. Mr. Nathan Brown (sorry to call you out like this home boy, but you will be a-ight/ all right). I have known Nate for a little more than 20 years and my observations of him have been unchanged in all that time. Whenever I see Nate play, his energy gives my spirit a humongous smile. I get chill bumps on my arm as I see and hear him laying down a groove and smiling as he does his job. It does not matter if it's Blues, Jazz, R&B, Funk, or whatever - he does his job in the most positive and effective way. It always looks like he was meant to play bass. I don't know anything else he does besides playing bass, but when I see Nate, I always think bass. Nate will demonstrate some of the exercises in this book, either on his website or YouTube. He has lots of very nice music and it would be a very good idea to check him out. By the way, did I mention that he is a "Detroit Native?"

The other day, Leroy was talking to Nate. "Hey, Nate - I heard Tony was writing some kind of book about Jazz or something. I'll see if I can borrow a copy from the library or get one on eBay or something."

Nate Brown, Native Detroit Bassist

The second example of a bassist doing what a bassist is supposed to do is Cecil McBee, Jr. In this case, as my mother used to say, "The apple don't fall far from the tree." Most of you already know the deal with Cecil McBee, Sr., but right now let's talk about Jr. He is another great player who can seriously cover any style of music. But I'm going to let another cat out of the bag. When you watch Cecil play, here's an inside scoop. When you see him curl up his bottom lip as if he's about to whistle, that's a sign that he's about to drop a really big musical bomb on you. He's going to really hurt you, so at that point I just shake my head and laugh. These examples and many others helped me understand what Milt meant when he said that we don't choose the instrument - it chooses us. This could also be a clue as to why Milt's fellow musicians gave him the nickname "the Judge."

Cecil McBee, Jr., San Diego Bassist

Exercise # 10   Whole Tone Scales

Since this scale is constructed of whole steps only, after building it, you will see that the notes are going to repeat themselves. The whole tone scale has the interval that naturally gives you a raised 5th, which is in the Augmented chord. It would be a good idea to practice this scale to become familiar with its sound and how you construct augmented chords.

The A Whole Tone Scale: A B C# D# F G A

"We should always practice patience. However, the best time to practice patience is when others around you don't practice patience. Sometimes I wish that others could be patient with me."

- Leroy

Hydra -a persistent or many-sided problem that presents new obstacles as soon as one aspect is solved.

I like to envision the road we travel along our musical journey as a hydra. As soon as we jump one hurdle there's another one coming right at you.

There's always going to be someone at a different level than yourself. Many times I hear remarks like, "He's the best," "He's the funkiest," or whatever. For me, I practice every day just to be a better person than I was the previous day. I don't participate in conversations where there's a comparison of levels of talent or anything else. To me, there's no best and no worst. Every person is unique and the best. We all bring something to the table in our own way. I remember Milt sharing a story with me about a situation that took place between him and Charles Mingus. You could possibly look that up online, but like Morgan Freeman said in the movie, Lean On Me, "That's all I'm gonna say about that!" The way Milt dealt with this situation is the way I prefer to handle anything similar to this that comes my way. I think Damian Erskine says it well:

"Never worry about how much there is to learn. We all exist within a spectrum and there will always be somebody below and above you. Don't compare yourself to others, but instead put all of your energy into just trying to be a little better tomorrow than you were yesterday. Knowledge comes in small steps. Those who go the furthest are those who just keep their heads down and focus on continuing to take those small steps, one after another. The secret to moving fast is to move slowly but steadily and with intention."

-Damian Erskine

Damian Erskine, Bassist

What I have noticed over the years is that it's best to stay open, because you can gain knowledge from every source you encounter. A great deal of the things that I've learned happened to have come from Leroy. However, sometimes things come with a price. What I mean by that is that it takes somewhat of a skill to separate, sort, and then absorb things from Leroy. At times, he's the coolest person you can meet. At other times, he's a handful. One of the things he mentioned to me that I continue to realize in my life is that we can learn from everyone we meet. If we are tuned in to what is actually going on in our daily life, we can learn something from each and every person we meet daily. Musicians, artists, and other talented people usually have several gifts - some of them they might not even be aware of. Have you ever noticed that sometimes your favorite actor/actress can also sing, dance, or play piano? I usually ask a new bassist that I'm sharing information with what they do or have done as a profession prior deciding to take up the bass. After I get their response, I often mention that, to whatever degree you did whatever you did, that is the exact degree of a bassist that you will become. I believe most things are either closely related or are the same, just the titles change. One example could be that, if you are a doctor, then the seriousness and attention you place on your medical studies will be just about at the same level of your bass studies. I have seen it way too many times for this just to be a coincidence. If you are a scientist, then you will have a tremendous amount of curiosity about your musical theory studies. Working on the exercises in this book or any other book for that matter should encourage you to look further to see what's next. I know a great deal of musicians that learn everything by ear and get stuck at a wall. Sometimes they stay at the wall and are not honest with themselves about going further. They stay there and never move forward. The majority of us musicians will NOT go to a Berklee or Julliard. We just learn what we learn from whatever source is available. Sometimes we end up better off in the long run.

"Every Person you meet each day is your teacher. If you are in tune [E A D G] there is something you can learn from each and every person you encounter."

- Leroy

Music Listening Exercise

There's a listening exercise that I like to do very often. It takes two or more people to really have fun with this. Get a pencil and paper, and then choose a song that is not really popular, or a version that is not very familiar. Have each person listen to the tune and write down everything that stood out to them or everything they liked about the song. For example, people might comment on the tone of the bass or the choice of notes or the space that was created by any of the musicians. After listening, exchange notes and see if anyone was able to hear something that you did not notice. Then, listen again. We all hear differently and pay attention to different things. This is a great opportunity to learn something new. If the other person plays a different instrument, that might be even better. Maybe a sax player or keyboard player hears sequences that we bassists don't really pay attention to. Maybe there is a unique way the phrase resolved. Once we take note of anything new and different, we can add it to our arsenal of things we can use.

"Listening is a major key to Survival."

Josh Chang, San Diego Bassist

At one point, after years of studying music, I noticed that, among all my senses, my sense of hearing was the strongest. This is not just related to hearing sounds. I also learned to investigate the nature of the sound being heard, whether it was in a musical setting or a conversation with someone. I remember a master musician from San Diego, pianist Carl Evans. Carl and I were on a gig and we played the tune Freedom Jazz Dance. He played the melody the first time and I played it the second time. I went through the melody playing the notes; however, when Carl played it, I could hear a big difference. His melody was almost like a voice. Afterwards I asked him what he was doing to make his melody sound completely different. Here's what he said: "Tony, when you learned the melody, did you just read it and then play it?" When I said yes, he mentioned that the song, which was written by Eddie Harris, was written as a reflection of a trip to Africa. The melody of the song was created to mimic a conversation in the African language. Carl asked me to sing the first line of the melody and then paused. After I did as he suggested, he told me to pretend that this first statement was a question. Then he told me to sing the second line as a response to the question, then the third and so on and so on. Once I sang and imagined the melody in this manner, I was able to play it with a whole new outlook. I should probably mention that Carl was such a great pianist that during any tune I could call out the name of ANY pianist and he would take a solo in that pianist's style. On one occasion during the sound check we were having sooooooo !!!! much fun that we played the sound check and ran straight into the actual gig start time without noticing. There are many melodies that you could sing or play in this kind of a call-response manner, and you will hear new ideas. Give it a try. I would be willing to bet that your sense of hearing is probably your strongest sense, too. There are things that we might not even be aware of that we do when we are listening to music. Some of us are able to hear and identify the tone, and at times the exact timbre. Some of us can even hear the intention of the chosen note. We can hear the emotion of the tone. There are some people who can even go as far as to be able to hear and distinguish the brand of bass that's being played. The list can continue.

Also on the subject of listening, I remember going to the Catalina Bar and Grill in LA to see my friend and fellow bassist, Eddie Resto. Eddie was playing with a host of heavy weights such as Alex Acuna and a handful of others. Eddie suggested that I get there early to listen to the sound check and get a good seat. I enjoyed the sound check just as much as the show, maybe even more. What stood out most during the sound check were the interactions between the musicians. I could feel the comradery between them. What I also noticed immediately was the unique manner in which Eddie was playing the bass lines. I could tell that he was doing two things at the same time. He was playing the bass line, but at the same time he was also listening to what was being presented by the other musicians in the band. Once the show started, I could hear the adjustments he made to his bass line so that he complemented each tune. His lines were very accurate and precise. Eddie was not over playing or underplaying. That is the sign of a master musician. This goes for a musician playing any instrument, and how we deal with the everyday life issues as well. We can take the time and try to find that space where we are not doing too much or too little. We can manage our responses after thinking a bit more before responding.

"Absence of Evidence is not Evidence of Absence."

Eddie Resto, West Coast Bassist

Exercise # 11   Diminished 7th chords

There are a lot of ways to practice with diminished chords that will help you improve your understanding of music theory. First, practice spelling the diminished 7th chords, both on paper and on the bass. There are times when you see that a diminished chord creates a chromatic flow between two or more chords. At other times, the diminished 7th chord is a tri-tone substitution that creates a half step motion between two or three chords. I usually practice diminished chords around the circle of fourths, or I move them in minor thirds.

Another thing that I like to practice is to create a groove using only diminished chords. Please refer to exercise #8, which uses the diminished scale as a foundation. Check out some of the older recordings of Victor Bailey, who would sometimes play a diminished line that might make you cry and want to burn your bass. Another thing that I learned from Leroy was that slow and fast are equally good, so start slow, and take it wherever it goes naturally.

When you are listening to the chord changes of a tune, usually the strongest tone coming to you is the one you should follow. That strong tone is most likely going to be your best indication of where the harmony and melody are heading. It might also be a good idea to see what the 3rd is, because the 3rd can be very important in Major, minor, and diatonic chords. Check each note of a chord individually to find what each note means harmonically. One of the best ways to learn a tune is to just hear where the song goes harmonically in your head. Listening to phrases to see what happens at the end of the phrase is also very helpful. Listen to the very last note, then listen to the next phrase and the last note of that phrase. Listen to sequences played by other instruments. I really enjoy listening to the horn players and the sequences they use. At one point I listened to Cannonball Adderley's sax lines for an extended period, which I later realized turned out to be two years. One thing that this taught me was to try playing the same sequence over different chords that are consecutive, like over two-five-ones.

After you are able to do this, it will be very easy to create multiple nice sounding bass lines. With this approach, you will be able to create a bass line without having to be stuck trying to follow each chord. One of the ways to know if a bass player is listening to the harmony is to check out if he or she is consistently trying to arpeggiate each and every chord. By going down this road, you will not be able to relax. You will not even be able to sneeze, cough or say hello to someone close enough to recognize. If you say hello or take your eyes off the chart you will immediately lose your place in the music. Please don't let it be a fast tune with several chords, because you most likely will be setting yourself up for failure. When it comes to these types of things, getting better comes with practice and patience, but first of all you have to have the awareness and be approachable and teachable. There are many whose egos are just too big to be bothered with any of this, so they continue to not be true to themselves. Have you ever noticed that if you are a great musician, other musicians will not hesitate to tell you so? In the case of a not-so-great sounding musician, there will be hesitation for a fellow musician to pull you up on this. Some musicians even refuse to comment for fear of losing a future gig. This is definitely not fair or cool, but it happens.

Exercise # 12   Moving chromatic Diminished chords and resolving them

Practice moving the diminished chords upwards and then downwards chromatically. Also, practice moving from the diminished chord, resolving to a minor 7th chord. You will see this a lot. Some examples are C#dim resolving to D-minor 7 or Eb dim resolving to D-minor 7.

Exercise #13   Multiple chord work

Select one note and then build every chord you can think of. For this exercise, we'll again use A as the root. I like to use a nice swinging drumbeat at a slow tempo, then gradually increase the tempo. Once you feel comfortable, increase the tempo until the wheels fall off (in other words, until you are not able to cleanly keep up). Below is a list of chords you can use and should be able to arpeggiate.

A Major 7
A Major 7 #11
A minor 7
A minor 9
A diminished 7
A augmented 7
A Major 6
A sus4
A minor 7b5
A Dom 7
A Dom 7b9
A 13

You will be surprised how many new ideas will come into your head as a result of doing this. Most likely, you will have fun too. You could also try adding the 6th to a chord for a fuller sound to both the one and four chords.

Exercise # 14   Permutations

A permutation is a major or fundamental change based primarily on rearrangement of the notes in the chord.

If you are a math or science person, this next exercise will be right up your alley and you will not have to work as hard as the rest of us to understand it. I recently befriended a scientist / bassist out of Detroit, and I'm sure she could create a blueprint for this exercise in her sleep. I will just explain it. Let's start with a Major 7 chord. There are four notes in the chord. Rearrange those four notes and come up with as many combinations as possible using only those four notes. Afterwards, play those different combinations and see what your ears like, then add that to your vocabulary of patterns to choose from. Subsequently, move to the other chords listed above. This can take a long time to complete, so don't be in a rush. When it comes to these types of things, I just call them bass "projects." Then, on rainy days when I sit down to practice, I have several projects to choose to work on, as opposed to just picking up the bass to entertain myself. Try not to confuse permutations with inversions. When you invert the chords, the chord tones stay in order. When you use permutations, you can rearrange the notes in as many different combinations as possible. Once you have several ideas stored in your musical vocabulary, you can call them up whenever needed. One thing I often find myself doing when playing tunes that I am not very familiar with is to go through the tune almost on autopilot using ideas that I have, since it doesn't require too much thought. While playing the tune, I am simultaneously studying the chords and harmony, looking for better ways to connect the dots. By the second chorus, I'll be in better shape to explore the tune even more.

There are several bass players that I sit down with to share different ideas and information. There have been times that I noticed uncomfortable vibes that arose from musicians when they were not too happy with another musician's ability to communicate with them, either through the music or through a theoretical discussion. This I have seen time and time again and the reason is usually a lack of musical respect that one will receive from fellow musicians. It would be better if the other musicians would just come out and tell you that your playing needs some help, or actually tell you what you need to work on. Sometimes, if there's an abundance of arrogance on board, the band leader will start to hurl insults. Insults for most are usually not the best fix. I can say that on more than one occasion I have used the negative energy from an insult that was thrown at me and turned it into a positive. However, an inexperienced musician might become insulted and embarrassed. My preferred way of helping with this is to immediately share different ideas and minor corrections whenever this takes place. I've been in the company of bassists that I may ask a certain question or pose a situation that might arise and place them in a difficult situation. My reason for this is to prepare them for such an unlikely situation, with hopes they can be prepared to deal with such. That way, if it happens on the gig or in rehearsal, they can deal with it better. The more we experience, the more we can learn, and the more prepared we will be.

"When it rains, look for rainbows. When it's dark, look for stars."
- Oscar Wilde

"Music is how you tell the story of your life journey."

Lamont "Terry" Battle, Baltimore Bassist

Exercise # 15   Moving from the 1 chord

Practice a nice medium tempo walking bass line moving from the one chord. Since the one chord can pretty much move to any chord, create a nice smooth bass line that has the one chord moving to the two chord. Play this line until you feel comfortable with it, then play the one chord moving to the three chord and so on and so on.

"Just because I might not say anything or my response might not seem to make sense to you, don't think for one minute that I am not aware of your thoughts and feelings towards me. Don't get things twisted."

Leroy

I have heard many different opinions about what I am going to share with you next, and this is just my opinion. Some musicians, bass players to be more specific, feel that it's not really a good idea to sit down and practice with another bass player. Me, on the other hand, I think it's an excellent idea. This is just one of the many ways that one can learn to play better. There are many different approaches that you can experiment with, e.g. taking turns playing the melody, walking through a chorus, or playing in a call and response manner. One of the ways I was taught was to take a bass line and divide it into several sections, even though it's one bass line. When you divide up a bass line, both players would do better if they started out with a similar tone. The goal would be to have both bassists sounding like only one bassist. Another thing you can try is to have one bass player demonstrate a specific theme or idea and the second bassist should try to come close or even repeat what he or she is hearing right after hearing it. When we share and have a decent, mutual respect for our brother and sister bass players, it makes us better. When we can honestly support each other, things get better quickly. Some bassists feel the need to hold on tight to whatever it is they think they know. They might try to make it seem magical or mysterious. Forget about all that - when you put good vibes and energy out there it comes back multiplied.

Exercise # 16   Pentatonic mode 1

Let's start with the first mode of the pentatonic scale. We might as well continue to use A as the root. This scale is comprised of the following notes: A B C# E F#
Practice this scale slowly. You will notice that it has a completely different sound and feel to it, possibly because it has fewer notes and maybe because of the minor third. Take note of the shape of this scale. The shape and sound will help you transpose the scale to other keys. After you are comfortable playing it, transpose the scale to every key via the circle of fourths. As you will see, each mode of the pentatonic scale

has a different shape and sound.

Quiet Time

The benefits of having a little bit of quiet time can be priceless. I make an attempt to have quiet time every day. I usually get up around 4am every morning. There are many ways to take in some quiet time: some people pray, some meditate, some read. Some just sit and do absolutely nothing. For me, the answer is "D" – all of the above. Most of the time when I'm having my quiet time, during or immediately afterwards, new ideas and thoughts come into my head. Sometimes, answers to things I was trying to figure out come to me. There is a strange magic that happens as a result of taking quiet time. You can really tap into some good things. Over the past few years, I have been digging deeply into my personal development. One of the many benefits I've noticed is that I see more, feel more, and enjoy more. Another thing I've noticed is that my personal filters have lessened. What I mean by this is I have noticed that more feelings and energy are allowed to enter my spirit. This means that more good can easily enter, but also the not so good. As a result of this level of increased awareness I get a chance to see the not so good earlier and have the opportunity to file it in a deserving place where it does not continue to present a big problem. It might not be a bad idea to give it a try. You will most likely see similar results. There's a tune that I really enjoy listening to at a very low volume during quiet time entitled, I'll Just Wait and Pray, recorded by Joe Lovano on his Sounds of Joy album.

Another blessing that I had was playing numerous gigs with a great pianist, Carl Evans. Playing gigs with Carl were life lessons. One day while we were en route to our gig, Carl asked me, "Tony do you know where the best ideas and thoughts are?" "Nope!" I replied. "Right over there," he said, pointing to a graveyard we were passing. He then went on
to say that most great ideas go to the grave with people

because, for one reason or another, they never attempt to bring their ideas to fruition. One morning a few years ago I got the idea to start a band. A different type of band. A band where there would be several bass players, not playing at the same time. I decided to start a band with the regular group of bass players that I sit with each week and share techniques and ideas and approaches to playing. I believe that since experience is the best teacher, why not hire the best musicians available in town? I came up with my list of a supporting cast of experienced musicians and explained to them what I was aiming at accomplishing with this project - that the bass players in this band are up and coming and new to playing music in a live situation. I also mentioned that the concept is to help teach these bassists how to create and perform in a live setting. I started out with three bassists and helped them with three or four standard tunes. We had rehearsals to work on the music, and then we got gigs. Each bassist plays a set or a portion of a set. Then, I came up with an appropriate name for the band, "FLEX." The vibe and energy were really nice, and every performance was a positive learning experience for us all. Each bass player brought his or her own different energy to the stage. Flex still performs throughout San Diego today. Anyone reading this book is welcome to sit in on a tune and play, if you happen to be in San Diego. I am very sure you will enjoy yourself. Creating Flex is the closest I could do to continue to share the brotherly and sisterly love that we all have for our music. This is a direct result and example of what I learned from Milt Hinton. I am truly sure he is smiling. I still remember seeing him seated in the front row of the Skidmore Jazz Institute auditorium with his hat cocked to one side, cheering for me as I played. I was playing HIS BASS too. He taught me the tune and gave me his bass and said, "Go get 'em, judge."

Flex Band July 2021
Photography by Jan Fronek

Exercise # 17   Pentatonic mode 2
Take a look at the second mode of the A pentatonic scale, which is comprised of the following notes: B C# E F# A
This mode has a slightly different fingering than the first mode, which I like to call a box. Once again, please play it slowly and try to let this sound sink into your head.

"Write your story - don't let someone else write it. If you write it, you can determine the ending."

– My Grand Ma

Exercise # 18   Pentatonic mode 3
The third mode of the A pentatonic scale is comprised of the following notes: C# E F# A B
Play it slowly and let the sound sink into your head and the different fingering get into your fingers.

Being successful as a musician

I remember my friend Milt asking me who was my sponsor. I had no clue what he was talking about. So, I responded that I didn't have any type of sponsor. Milt immediately got quiet, and the look on his face kind of went blank. After a few minutes I asked him what indeed was a sponsor, and why was that even necessary. It was at this point that his face lit up and he smiled, glad to share with me his perspective on a sponsor. Milt went on to say that his wife Mona had always been his sponsor. He said a sponsor is someone who believes in you and what you are doing. He said a sponsor has absolutely nothing to do with a company or someone that endorses you from a monetary or equipment type of thing. He said that his wife Mona believed in him since day one. This he said is what kept him in a good place while out on the road traveling throughout the world. Just about every successful musician I know has some type of sponsor.

Exercise # 19   Pentatonic mode 4
The 4th mode of the A pentatonic scale consists of the following notes: E F# A B C# Once again, practice it slowly, listen carefully and memorize the fingering.

Exercise # 20   Pentatonic mode 5
The 5th mode of the pentatonic scale is used a lot in jazz. It is sometimes called the minor pentatonic scale. When you take a look at the fingering, you will immediately see how and why this sounds very nice over a minor chord. This one is my favorite.
The notes in the 5th mode of the A pentatonic scale are:
F# A B C# E.

> "When starting to practice, be eager like a deer trapped in a pen seeking to get out."
> In the middle be like a farmer during harvest not waiting for anything.
> "In the end be like a shepherd who has brought the flock home."
> -Paltrul Rinpoche's Sacred Word
> (as quoted in How to See Yourself As You Really Are By His Holiness, the Dalai Lama)

Conclusion

When it comes to music, the road to learning never ends. Similar to what my mom still tells me, when it comes to life, learning never stops. The good thing is that, if you grab a handful of life that you almost understand, you can go out and be successful. Always leave all the doors and windows open to allow fresh air/info/knowledge to enter. With this approach, you will always be a winner. The day that we think we know it all is the beginning of an unpleasant journey. Keep learning, be kind, and share, and we all will be ok.

There's an African proverb that says if you want to go fast go alone, but if you want to go far go together.

Thank you for being a part of Bass-ick Theory

-Tony Muhammad – GOD Bless

Note to Reginald: Hey, bro. I ain't one to spread rumors, but I heard that Brother Leroy is relocating to Detroit. He mentioned something about a bass group called the Detroit Bass Players. I don't know what to tell you bro, except good luck with that.

Zen Reinhardt, Detroit Bassist

Afterword

I have known Anthony "Tony" Muhammad for the last 47 years. My biological brother and dear friend, Manuel Brown, initially met Tony in the year of 1974. It was Manuel's freshman year at Southwestern Senior High School, located in our hometown of Baltimore, Maryland. Since the inception of Manuel's and Tony's friendship and brotherhood, Tony instantaneously became my mother's (Ms. Catherine Florence May Booker) son and my brother from another mother (Ms. Catherine McCleod). I am not a writer or musician, only an innate lover of music. So, when Tony selected me to write the Afterword for his most recent book, BASS-ICK THEORY VOLUME 02- CONVERSATIONS WITH LEROY- DETROIT EDITION, I immediately panicked. After the mental and emotional state of panic subsided, I discovered that I did not know Tony as well as I thought. The sudden uncontrollable fear that emerged within my inner physical existence as a result of Tony's request for me to author his Afterword had many origins. However, the primary source of my fear and anxiety was rooted in the fact that I knew very little about Tony's musical evolution and business associations from an entertainment point of view. In realizing that I did not know Tony as well as I thought, I accepted the fact that I needed to have a conversation with Leroy.

It was not until I learned to evoke and bring forth the spirit of Tony's fictional character Leroy that I discovered an unsung, world class bassist. Tony truly is a world class bassist with nearly fifty years of untold life lessons in music and actual accounts that are not reflected or shared in the pages of this book. His humble and respectful unwillingness to write about the various artists he has performed with officially or unofficially does not reflect his performance history and outstanding professional musical experience. Among these artists are Lonnie Liston Smith,
Dennis Chambers, Greg and Gary Grainger, Gregory Porter, Jeremy Pelt, Vinnie Falcone, Joe Piscopo and many others that

he humbly refuses to reveal.

With the assistance of Leroy, I unearthed the profundity of Tony's formal and informal musical education and the thought process/way of life that created an original strategy for self-sponsorship, which provides him with a peaceful and quality way of life. This strategy for self-sponsorship can also be explored and created by you, the reader. You must be willing to use your imagination and invent a personal strategy for self-sponsorship that is tailor-made specifically for yourself.

Leroy, an intellectual and musical giant who can be obnoxious and belligerent, is willing to physically brawl without delay if provoked in a manner that he deems disrespectful, musically or otherwise. In contrast, Tony is a man of humility, who will not boast or speak about the numerous intimate relationships and music connections that comprise his everyday life. From the lawn care professional to the billionaire financial investor, he can respectfully access unlimited expertise, resources, and assistance without a moment's hesitation, based on his humility and humanity. Tony's life's preference is to be a faceless face in the crowd, the master of deflecting accolades, acknowledgements and attention, the unknown musician who plays a walking bassline flawlessly and then mysteriously disappears into the audience after the band's last set.

There are twenty music practice exercises in this edition, which could be misinterpreted as the primary focus of the book. Furthermore, it was not until I talked with Leroy that I began to acquire a clearer understanding of Tony's writings and life philosophy. After speaking with Leroy and reading the manuscript, my perception of the book's message changed from basic music theory (prescriptive nonfiction) to a book of history, spirituality, music discovery and self-help manual. According to Leroy, "It's not only about knowing lyrics and theory intellectually, it's about knowing and understanding the permanent intelligence and reality of the universe, which exist within all living creatures, which sustains all life, including the origin and life of music." Trumpeter, Nicholas Payton, on his 2017 CD, AFRO CARIBBEAN MIXTAPE states, "Playing an instrument is a form of worship, and I've been worshipping all of my life."

In addition to the exercises, Tony provides philosophical quotes from noted musicians and his personal friend and music teacher, the late Mr. Milton John Hinton, who he came in contact with as a student while attending the summer jazz programs at Skidmore Jazz Institute, located in Saratoga Springs, New York. Tony also attended Peabody Preparatory of The Johns Hopkins University, Summer Program at Manhattan School of Music, Southwestern College (Chula Vista, California) and San Diego State University music programs. Regardless of his extensive list of formal institutional music training and exposure, nothing eclipsed the overall education he received from Mr. Hinton. The primary lesson Tony learned from Mr. Hinton is the importance of being consistently kind to all people, in conjunction with bass practice and playing.

Mr. Hinton was a double bassist, photographer and educator born June 23, 1910, in Vicksburg, Mississippi during the open hostility and violence of the Jim Crow era in the United States. Jim Crow laws were federal, state and local laws that enforced and forced racial segregation of black and white people in the Southern United States and throughout the nation. Jim Crow laws were not abolished until 1965. Mr. Hinton performed with Cab Calloway for seventeen years and was one of the first bassists to play a walking bassline.
He also played with Jabbo Smith, James Zutty Singleton, Art Tatum, Eddie South, Count Basie, Louis Armstrong, Dizzy Gillespie, Lionel Hampton, Benny Goodman, Clark Terry, Hank Jones and Branford Marsalis, too.

Tony's desire to grow as both a musician and music educator led him to a ninety-minute music encounter with Ms. Carol Kaye in what could be described as a bassist consultation. Ms. Kaye is considered one of the best and most productive recorded bass guitarists in rock and popular music, having played on an estimated ten thousand recordings in nearly a six-decade music career. During the year of 2020, Rolling Stone magazine acknowledged Ms. Kaye as number five on its list of the 50 greatest bassists of all time. Throughout the consultation, she provided Tony with methods to improve how to share his musical understanding with others when conducting bass lessons and directing musical ensembles, and concluded by providing him with a recording of the entire consultation, including a bass solo he performed for her in real time. With each portion of the solo that she determined needed improvement for his overall musical

evolution as a bassist, she politely requested that he cease playing for a moment, made a trip to her personal library, and returned with a book addressing the subject matter. Prior to returning with the book, she highlighted an excerpt that she wanted Anthony to read, focus on, and improve upon, musically. In all, Ms. Kaye made two to three individual walks to her library during that first and only consultation. A consummate learner who knows he can learn from everyone he meets, Tony took a great amount of musical education away from this experience and it has enhanced his ability to share what he knows.

From the year of 2007 until 2013, Tony served as the music director of the house band for Anthology, a notable music venue located in San Diego, California. During his tenure as music director, he personally recruited the very best professional musicians from the San Diego area. The original ensemble included singer Rebecca Jade, trumpeter Derek Cannon, guitarist Jeff Moore, drummer Russell Bizzett, tenor saxophonist John Rekevics, as well as pianists Kamau Kenyatta and Kevin Flournoy. After the closing of Anthology, Tony continues to write books, practice and play bass, recruit, and develop the best musical talent in the San Diego area, along with seasoned professional musicians. In fact,
he extends an open invitation to musicians from throughout the United States and the world to perform with his newly

established musical ensemble, The Flex Band (see Flex-band.com), when visiting the San Diego area.

In conclusion, it's clear to me that any reader who has access and influence on any level in the music industry, the halls of academia, and grassroot music organizations would be well-served by enlisting Tony as a music workshop guest speaker, university lecturer, music director trainer or just an old fashioned, down to earth homeboy willing to talk shop, musically. With his deep knowledge of music theory, extensive experience, and admirable personal traits, he could not fail to bring a very positive experience to all.

Daniel Brown Jr.,
Danny's and Catherine's Son

Daniel Brown, Jr.

Acknowledgments

My mother, Catherine McCleod – everything good that I am is because of you.

Resources

Flex-band.com

Nate Brown: nathanbrownonline.com

Michael Rais: michaelrais.com

Additional thanks to...

Helane Fronek for the many hours, as well as the heart and soul she put into both of my books. It is true that I wrote the books – and it was Helane who brought them to life.
For that, I am very grateful.

Theron Jacobs, whose expert computer skills perfectly translated my vision for the front and back covers. The cover introduces a book, and Theron's expertise created a unique frame that helped me honor the many bassists I admire.

And finally, my thanks go to the countless bassists and other musicians I have studied with, listened to, played with, or shared my own understanding of music with over the years. I have learned from each of you and consider you all to have been my teachers. I believe that as we continue to bring music into the world, we contribute to a richer and more beautiful society for all people to live in.

Made in United States
North Haven, CT
14 November 2021